IRELAND'S
WESTERN ISLANDS

Inishbofin, The Aran Islands, Inishturk,
Inishark, Clare & Turbot Islands

Pete Tierney, East End, Inishbofin

IRELAND'S
WESTERN ISLANDS

Inishbofin, The Aran Islands, Inishturk,
Inishark, Clare & Turbot Islands

JOHN CARLOS

The Collins Press

For all Irish islanders, especially those who
were dispossessed of their homelands

In memory of my uncle, Gerald Glynn,
an Aran disciple and keen photographer

The book is dedicated to my mother, Emmie, who encouraged me to use her simple
Kodak camera during our visits to Inis Mór in the mid-1960s. Her regard for the islands
and their people inspired me to return to the islands one day to carry out this project.

FIRST PUBLISHED IN 2014 BY
The Collins Press
West Link Park
Doughcloyne
Wilton
Cork

Reprinted 2014

A CIP record for this book is available from the British Library.

ISBN: 978-1-84889-205-7

Design and typesetting by Fairways Design
Typeset in Minion Pro/New Aster
Printed in Poland by Białostockie Zakłady Graficzne SA

ACKNOWLEDGEMENTS

My appreciation and gratitude go primarily to the islanders in realising this project, for their trust, support and patience. These photographs are created from that experience, and of knowing a warm and hospitable people.

I am very grateful to Vincent Browne, my former Editor at the *Sunday Tribune*, for his generosity in providing me with time from the newspaper to work on the photographs.

To Margaret and the late Miko Day, Kieran Day and Theresa Ryan for their generosity, support and hospitality on Inishbofin, and also to the following for their warm hospitality: Mary Day Lavelle and Olive Day, both formerly of Day's Hotel; the Murray family at the Doonmore Hotel; the Coyne family, Dolphin Hotel; Caroline Coyne, the Galley and Orla Day and Adrian Herlihy at Day's Bar. My appreciation also goes to the following: Marie Coyne, Inishbofin Heritage Museum; Simon Murray and the Inishbofin Arts Festival Committee; Pat and Dermot Concannon of Island Discovery ferries, Inishbofin; O'Grady's and O'Malley's ferry companies who service Clare Island and Inishturk; Michael Joe O'Halloran, Inishbofin, and his brother, Martin, Inishturk; Mary Catherine and Bill Heanue, Inishturk; the late Delia Concannon, John Concannon and Mary-Jo Prendergast, Inishturk, and John and Mary Moran, Clare Island.

The memorial to the Kansas students on p. 86 was sculpted by John Behan and initiated by Margaret Day, Inishbofin. I am grateful to Bobby Molloy, when he was Minister for Defence, and the Irish Air Corps for their help with the photograph on p. 92. The Inishbofin map drawn by Kieran Concannon and produced by the Inishbofin Heritage Project was very helpful.

My appreciation and thanks go also to the following: Treasa Hernon Joyce, the late Bridget Hernon and the staff at Kilmurvey House, Inis Mór (it was at this fine guesthouse that I first developed my interest in photography). To the staff of the Dún Aonghasa Heritage Centre, Kilmurvey, Inis Mór; Mick and Barbara O'Connell, Inis Mór; the staff and crews of Aran Island Ferries; the Aer Arann crews and ground staff including Michael and Peggy Hernon, Inis Mór; Rúairí Ó Conghaile, Tigh Rúairí and Johnny and Úna Mc Donagh, Inis Oírr.

Some place names were gleaned from the *Folding Landscapes* map, Oileáin Árann by Tim Robinson. I also consulted Richard Scott's book, *The Galway Hookers*, for caption information for the photograph on p. 200.

Thank you to Joe O'Shaughnessy and Billy Stickland for your goodwill and support; to Dave O'Connell, Group Editor and David Hickey, Group CEO, *The Connacht Tribune*, Galway, whose newspaper published photographs from the early Aran and Inishbofin work; to Gordon Standing of *The Irish Times*, for publishing the early Aran photographs; to Letitia Pollard, former editor of *Ireland of the Welcomes,* and Sonya Perkins, former editor-in-chief of *The World of Hibernia*, for publishing selections of the Inishbofin photographs. A selection of the Inishbofin work also appeared in *Inishbofin and Inishark*, published by James Morrissey, Crannóg Books. I am grateful to Jonathan Williams and Gerry Dawe for their contribution in

the initial days of the project. Thank you to Sharon Duffy of the Davitt Photo Centre, Salthill, Galway, who produced the work-prints for the project. A special thanks to my publishers, The Collins Press, for bringing this project to fruition.

I also pay special tribute to the inspiring collaborative works of author and storyteller John Berger and Jean Mohr and also the photography of Paul Strand.

John Carlos

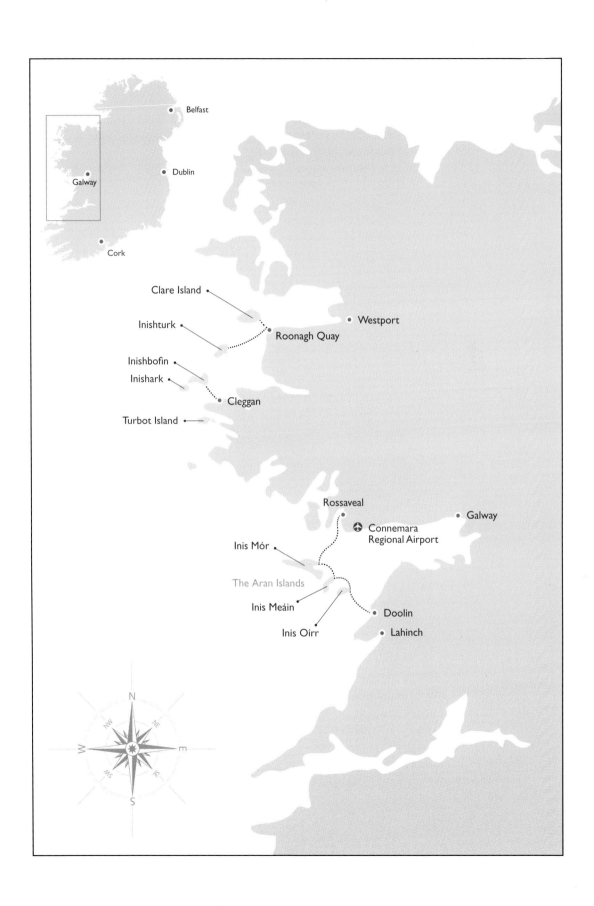

INTRODUCTION

This book is a celebration of the islanders of Inishbofin and the Aran Islands: Inis Mór, Inis Meáin and Inis Oírr, County Galway. It includes the islands of Inishturk and Clare Island, County Mayo, and also honours the people of Inishark and Turbot Island, County Galway, who were evacuated from their islands by the Irish government in 1960 and 1978 respectively.

The work reflects on disappearing traditions and culture in a society increasingly consumed by materialism, information technology and celebrity culture.

The sequences, which suggest a form of narration, draw on many elements to create a unity of opposites: people, wild flowers, youth, landscapes, home, religious icons, work, seascapes, animals, fish, rocks, love and loss. People and nature are intricately woven to portray their relationship with the islands, and the complexity of their lives therein.

The book is not an attempt in any way to define the islands or their people, but rather, to preserve a memory of the islanders and their homelands. Although the work spans almost fifty years, the photographs barely touch the surface of such a rich and diverse culture.

The population of our offshore islands has dwindled from 35,000 in the 1800s to fewer than 3,000 today. Between the 1950s and 1970s, several communities off the western seaboard were displaced from their islands, resulting in the destruction of their culture and identity.

The lack of adequate investment in employment incentives, even during our economically buoyant times, has drained the population on islands such as Inishturk. In 1985 there were thirty pupils in the island's National school; in 2014 there were three.

There are few temples or shrines honouring Irish islanders. There are, however, a myriad of memorials dedicated to their folk and fishermen lost at sea.

Apart from earlier visits to Inishbofin since 1976, the main thrust of the work was undertaken there and on the surrounding islands from 1992 until 2011. The photographs in Aran were made at various intervals from 1965 until 2013.

East End village, Inishbofin

Bernie O'Halloran and Síog, Inishbofin

Michael Ó Conghaile and his sister, Sarah Crowe, Inis Oírr, Aran

Maeve Flaherty, Gort na gCapall, Inis Mór, Aran

Máirtín Éanna Conneely with the replica he made of his father's trawler,
Iúda Naofa, *Sruthán, Inis Mór, Aran*

An Sunda Caoch, Inis Mór, Aran

Dún Dúchathair, Inis Mór, Aran

Teach Synge, Inis Meáin, Aran: a museum dedicated to the life and work of the celebrated playwright John Millington Synge

Gort na gCapall village, Inis Mór, Aran

The Shamrock guesthouse and Dún Formna castle, Inis Oírr, Aran

Owen Coyne, Middlequarter, Inishbofin

The MV Plassy, which ran aground in 1960 on Inis Oírr, Aran

The Naomh Éanna *ferry at Inis Oírr, Aran*

Ros Éinne *trawler in Cill Éinne, Inis Mór, Aran*

(L-r): Bill Heanue and Martin O'Halloran, Inishturk

Blessing of the bay, Inishbofin

Madonna and Child, Inishbofin Church

The signal light tower at the mouth of Inishbofin harbour

John Day, Middlequarter, Inishbofin

Kilronan harbour, Inis Mór, Aran

Gerry Moran, Inishbofin　　　　　*Thomas Cunnane, Inishbofin*

(L-r): Francis Day, Máirtín Lavelle, George Lacey and Enda Concannon, Inishbofin

Pat Coyne, Clossy, Inishbofin

Baile an Teampaill, Inis Meáin, Aran

Roofing a house, Inis Meáin, Aran

Relegated to the farm shed, Inis Meáin, Aran

Herding sheep, Inis Meáin, Aran

Sheep shears and wool, Inishbofin

Simon Murray, North Beach, Inishbofin

Ann Day, Fawnmore, Inishbofin

John O'Halloran, Claddaghduff, Connemara, reeking the hay on Coyne's farm, Inishbofin

Henry Kenny, East End, Inishbofin

Jarleth Ward and his nephew John Ward, Inishbofin

Tommy Burke and Louisburgh Fergal 1st, Inishbofin

Andrew Concannon, Fawnmore, Inishbofin

Sonny's old hay rake, Kilmurvey House, Inis Mór, Aran

James Folan, Kilronan, Inis Mór, Aran

Cartwheel, Kilnurvey, Inis Mór, Aran

Bartley Gill, Kilronan, Inis Mór, Aran

Mac Phait Sheáin Ó Conghaile, Creig a Chéirín, Inis Mór, Aran

Tom Hernon and Molly, Kilmurvey, Inis Mór, Aran

Funeral, Cill Éinne, Inis Mór, Aran

Horse cart and cottage ruin, Inis Mór, Aran

Thatching, Inis Mór, Aran

Currach, Inis Mór, Aran

Rendezvous at Kilmurvey as Aran men make their way to work on Inis Mór

Michael Schofield, Inishbofin

James Coyne and his daughter, Maeve, Inishbofin

Andrew Murray and his son, Luke, North Beach, Inishbofin

Michael Joe O'Halloran and his nephew, Shane Prendergast, Inishbofin

On the beach, Inis Oírr, Aran

Treasa Hernon, Kilmurvey, Inis Mór, Aran

Treasa Hernon Joyce and her daughter, Ailsa, Kilmurvey, Inis Mór

Ailsa and Noel Joyce, Kilmurvey, Inis Mór

Teresa Abeyta with Sailor and Genie, Inishbofin

Tortoiseshell butterflies, Inishbofin

Pat Concannon and Nikola Jones, Low Road, Inishbofin

The living room, Kilmurvey House, Inis Mór, Aran

Kevin and Seán Abeyta, East End, Inishbofin

Tazzie (front), Aengus and Caroline Murray, Fawnmore, Inishbofin

First Holy Communicants Aoife King and Simon Cloonan, Inisbofin

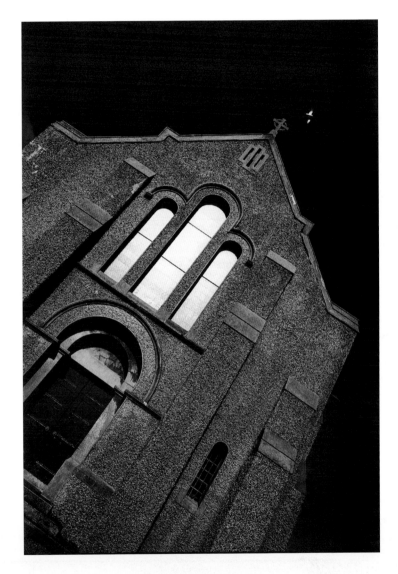

The church, Inishbofin

*Fr Declan Carroll, the last full-time priest on Inishbofin, pictured before
he departed from the island in 2001*

Kieran Day and Theresa Ryan, Clossy, Inishbofin, on their wedding day in Galway

Michael Day, Clossy, Inishbofin

Blackberry flower, Inishbofin

Kitty Concannon, Low Road, Inishbofin

Blackberry fruit, Inishbofin

Margaret Day and her grandson, Conor Day, Inishbofin

Laura Hopkins from Westport in her grandparents' house on Inishturk

Bridget Dirrane, Inis Mór, at 106 years. A member of Cumann na mBan, the republican women's organisation, she went on hunger strike when in Mountjoy Jail. She became a nurse in the early 1900s and after her arrest while on duty in the Dublin home of a nationalist sympathiser, she infuriated the police at the Bridewell station by dancing and singing in Irish. She married an Aran Islander, Ned Dirrane, in Boston, where she joined the Democratic Party and campaigned for John F. Kennedy. She drove a Chevrolet Bel Air to cover her nationwide nursing assignments while in the US. After Ned died, she returned to Aran and married his brother, Patrick. When he in turn died, she had her two wedding rings bonded together. Bridget died on New Year's Eve 2003 at the age of 109.

Inishbofin harbour as seen from Eileen Coyne's home

Fence post, Dumhach, Inishbofin

Kilronan harbour, Inis Mór, Aran

Trawler skeleton, Kilronan harbour, Inis Mór, Aran

An Sunda Caoch, Inis Mór, Aran

Tourists sailing to Inis Mór, Aran

Memorial to Kansas students, the Stags, Inishbofin

Bog-water plant, Inishbofin

Michael Burke, East End, Inishbofin

Desmond O'Halloran, the Pound Road, Inishbofin

Pete Conneely, Baile an Fhormna, Inis Oírr, Aran

The Dún Aengus *ferry sailing to Inishbofin*

*The remains of Pete Burke being airlifted by helicopter during
rough seas to Inishbofin*

Islanders collecting supplies from the Naomh Éanna *ferry for Inis Meáin, Aran*

Rock art, Inis Mór, Aran

Funeral, Inishbofin church

Sheep skull, limestone and flora, Inis Mór, Aran

Michael Gibbons, archaeologist, on the south coast of Inis Mór, Aran

Oarsmen returning from the sea with their currach on Inis Oírr, Aran

Limestone terraces, Gort na gCapall, Inis Mór, Aran

Waiting for the ferry, Aran

Transporting seaweed, Kilmurvey, Inis Mór, Aran

Departing Inis Oírr, Aran, for the Naomh Éanna *sailing to Galway*

Disembarking from the Naomh Éanna *for Inis Oírr, Aran*

Aer Arann flying into Inis Meáin, Aran

Pony traps and bus approaching Dún Aonghasa fort, Kilmurvey, Inis Mór, Aran

Máire Pháidín Uí Maolchiaráin and Juno, Inis Meáin, Aran

Gaelgóirí arrive for their three-week Irish language course on Inis Oírr, Aran

*Treasa Ní Fhátharta at her childhood home on Inis Meáin, Aran, which she has
dedicated as a museum to the playwright John Millington Synge*

Baile an Teampaill, Inis Meáin, looking towards the coast of Clare

Mural, Kilronan, Inis Mór, Aran

Tourists on Dún Aonghasa fort, Inis Mór, Aran

Eochaill, Inis Mór, Aran

Tourists on Dún Aonghasa fort, Inis Mór, Aran

After Mass, Inishbofin

Ferry sailing from Inis Mór, Aran

Noel Joyce, Kilmurvey House, Inis Mór, Aran

Wild flower and limestone, Inis Mór, Aran

Frances Cunnane, Inishbofin

John Michael Coyne, Inishbofin

John and Mary Moran, Clare Island

Wendy Maher's dog Lady, East End, Inishbofin

James and Patsy Coyne with Diver, Westquarter, Inishbofin

Laurence Ward, Inishbofin

John Lavelle, Inishbofin

Day's Bar at Christmas, Inishbofin

Máirtín Cloonan, Inishbofin

Football on Dumhach Strand, Inishbofin

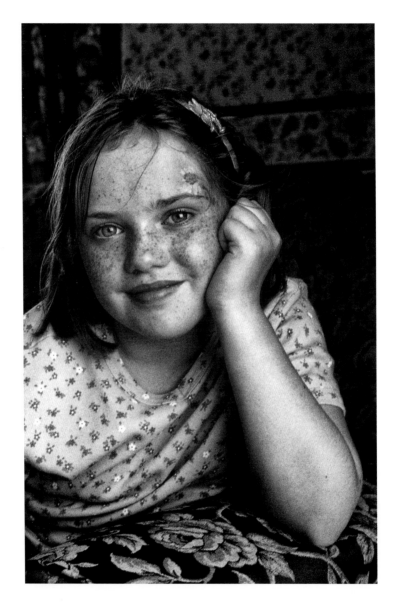

Aisling Flaherty, Gort na gCapall, Inis Mór, Aran

David Lavelle, Inishbofin

Peadar King, Inishbofin

(L–r): Vivienne Lavelle and her mother, Nickie, East End, Inishbofin

Bog wood, Clare Island

Heather roots, Inishbofin

Noel Schofield, Fawnmore, Inishbofin

Church icons being stored in one of the former homes on Inishark

Cromwell's Barracks, Inishbofin

The ruined church, Inishark

Christmas, Dolphin Hotel, Inishbofin

Gaelgóir student, Inis Oírr, Aran

Visiting nun, Inis Oírr

Anne Burke, Fawnmore, Inishbofin

Election poster, Inis Mór, Aran

Aidan Day, Fawnmore, Inishbofin

The Roving Swan *at Kilronan harbour, Inis Mór, Aran*

John Greene on the Dún Aengus *ferry, Inishbofin*

Banríon na Farraige ('Queen of the Sea') *ferry entering Inis Meáin harbour, Aran*

(L-r): Leo Lavelle, Séamus and Dermot Concannon and Jim Prendergast, Inishbofin

Passing the Leenane Head, *Inishbofin*

Inishturk harbour

John and Delia Concannon, Inishturk

Blessing, Inishbofin

Bridget McCann, North Beach, Inishbofin

John and Marie Abeyta, East End, Inishbofin

Kitty King, High Road, Inishbofin

John Cunnane and Sam loading turf on Inishbofin

Declan O'Halloran, Westquarter, Inishbofin

Digging potatoes, Kilmurvey, Inis Mór, Aran

Brendan O'Halloran, Fawnmore, Inishbofin

Kilronan Pier, Inis Mór, Aran

Francis O'Halloran, Westquarter, Inishbofin

Lobster, Inishbofin

Carmel and Liam Byrne, East End, Inishbofin

Kitchen, Fawnmore, Inishbofin

Mary Guckian Day, former nurse, Inishbofin

Window at Christmas, East End, Inishbofin

Mary Gallagher Burke, East End, Inishbofin

Avril Day, Inishbofin

Ian Day, Inishbofin

Sarah McCabe, Clare Island

Michelle Conneely, Sruthán, Inis Mór, Aran

Paddy and Margaret Murray, Inishbofin

Jim and Ann Prendergast, Inishbofin

Aisling O'Malley and her father,
Michael Bob, Clare Island

Caimin Coyne and his sister,
Cliodhna, Inishbofin

Leo Lavelle, East End, Inishbofin

Paddy Joe Heanue and Pup, Inishturk

Awaiting the arrival of the ferry, Inis Oírr, Aran

An Trá and beyond, Baile an tSéipéil, Inis Oírr, Aran

Kilronan, Inis Mór, Aran

Padraig Kilmartin and Brownie, Inis Mór, Aran

Gaelgóirí students depart for the Naomh Éanna *ferry to Galway, following their Irish language studies on Inis Oírr, Aran*

A cow being winched from the hold of the Naomh Éanna *ferry to be towed by currach into Inis Oírr, Aran*

Islanders transporting a Honda 50 by currach from the ferry into Inis Meáin, Aran

Pony and trap, Kilmurvey, Inis Mór, Aran

Kathleen O'Halloran Morrison and Cathy Coyne, Middlequarter, Inishbofin

Alice O'Halloran and her mother, Mary, North Beach, Inishbofin

Cottage at Sruthán, Inis Mór, Aran

Cottages, East End, Inishbofin

Miko Day, Old School House, Inishbofin

Frank O'Halloran, Westquarter, Inishbofin

Station of the Cross, Inishbofin church

John Dory, Inishturk

Wild iris leaves, Inishturk

Bás don Iasc Mara ('death to sea fish'), a play on the initials of Bórd Iascaigh Mhara, the Irish Sea Fisheries Board, which has come up against strong opposition from the people of Inis Oírr, Aran, to the Board's plans for a major fish farm, the largest of its kind in Europe, due for development near the island

Multilingual anti-litter sign, Inis Oírr, Aran

Blackberry briars, Inishturk

Crucifix, Inishbofin church

Sailor on Dumhach Strand, Inishbofin

Cemetery, Inis Mór, Aran

Port Bhéal an Dúin, Inis Mór, Aran

(L–r): Patrick Joseph O'Toole and Pat Heaney, Inishturk

Inishark pier

Inishbofin harbour and High Island

Paddy O'Halloran sailing the Leenane Head, *Inishbofin*

The American Mór *hooker, once used for the turf trade from*
Connemara to the Aran Islands

Marine rescue helicopter on a training exercise with Aran Island Ferries to Inis Mór, Aran

Marine rescue training on the ferry to Inis Mór, Aran

A cow being lowered by winch from the Naomh Éanna *ferry to be towed by currach into Inis Oírr, Aran*

Paddy Cantwell, former captain of the Naomh Éanna *ferry
on Kilronan pier, Inis Mór, Aran*

Eamonn Day and his baby brother, Alan, High Road, Inishbofin

Rúairí Ó Conghaile transporting a cow from the ferry to Inis Oírr, Aran

Micheál Ó Domhnaill, Inis Meáin, Aran

A horse being lowered from the ferry on to Kilronan pier, Inis Mór, Aran

A cow being manoeuvred to the ferry at Kilronan for transport to Galway

Transporting sheep to Damhoileán, Inishbofin

Margaret O'Halloran, Westquarter, Inishbofin

Flora and foliage, Inishturk

Bunamullen Bay, Inishbofin

Marie Coyne, Middlequarter, Inishbofin

Máirtín D'Arcy, East End, Inishbofin

Honeysuckle amid the blackberry briars, Inis Mór, Aran

Aoife O'Toole, Baile Thiar, Inishturk

Burnet Rose, Inis Mór, Aran

Paddy Quinn entertaining tourists on the way to Dún Aonghasa fort, Inis Mór, Aran

The American Bar, Kilronan, Inis Mór, Aran

Inishbofin musicians: Michael Joe O'Halloran, bodhrán, Francis O'Halloran, fiddle and Paddy Joe King on the button accordion, known in traditional Irish music circles as 'the box'

Quentin O'Halloran, Fawnmore, Inishbofin

Philip Coyne, East End, Inishbofin

Shags nesting on the cliff face at Uaimh na gCáilleach, Inishbofin

Chevaux-de-frise defence stones, Dún Aonghasa fort, Inis Mór, Aran

Gort na gCapall, Inis Mór, Aran

Kilmurvey, Inis Mór, Aran

(L–r): Coleman King and Jason Prendergast, Low Road, Inishbofin

Festie McCann, North Beach, Inishbofin

Observing the arrival and departure of visitors to Inis Oírr, Aran

Barbara Day, The Gáirdín, Inishbofin

Jamesie Cunnane, The Bogs, Inishbofin

Kilronan, Inis Mór, Aran

*(L-r): Fr Padraig Standún, author and former parish priest, and
Peadar Mór Ó Conghaile, Inis Meáin, Aran*

After Mass, Inishbofin

Farmers strimming meadows on Inis Meáin, Aran

Tourists on Dún Aonghasa fort, Inis Mór, Aran

Aran men waiting for the ferry

Breandán Ó hÉithir, writer, broadcaster and native of Inis Mór, Aran

Aer Arann airfield, Cill Éinne, Inis Mór, Aran

Gaelgóirí depart Inis Oírr, Aran, following their Irish-language studies

Leaving Inis Meáin, Aran

The church, Inis Oírr, Aran

The Ceol na Farraige *('Music of the Sea') ferry docking at Inis Oírr, Aran*

Dennis Burke on his Confirmation Day with his family and
Archbishop Joseph Cassidy, Inishbofin

The Queen of Aran *ferry sailing out of Inishbofin harbour*

An Trá, Inis Oírr, Aran

Paddy Joe O'Halloran sailing the Leenane Head, *Inishbofin*

Mary Burke and her daughter, Aisling, Fawnmore, Inishbofin

Mending fishing nets on Turbot Island

Philomena Murray, from Inishark, who now lives in England

One of the old homes vacated on Inishark in 1960

Theresa McGuigan, teacher, in her school on Inishturk, which comprises just three children (l–r):
Ryan, Nathan, and Katelyn Heanue

National school, Turbot Island

Theresa McGuigan sets sail for Inishturk from Roonagh Pier, with Croagh Patrick,
one of Ireland's sacred mountains, in the background